TWO HALVES OF THE WORLD APPLE

TWO HALVES OF THE WORLD APPLE

Poems by Yang Ke

Translation by Denis Mair, Chao, Simon Patton, Ouyang Yu, and Ning Yang

Foreword by Jonathan Stalling

UNIVERSITY OF OKLAHOMA PRESS : NORMAN

LIBRARY OF CONGRESS CATALOGING-IN-PUBLICATION DATA

Names: Yang, Ke, 1957– author. | Mair, Denis C., translator. | Chao, 1964–
 translator. | Patton, Simon, translator. | Ouyang, Yu, 1955– translator. |
 Stalling, Jonathan, writer of foreword.
 Title: Two halves of the world apple : poems / by Yang Ke ; translation by
 Denis Mair, Chao, Simon Patton, Ouyang Yu, and Ning Yang ; foreword by
 Jonathan Stalling.
 Description: Norman : University of Oklahoma Press, 2017.
 Identifiers: LCCN 2017003538 | ISBN 978-0-8061-5759-7 (pbk. : alk. paper)
 Subjects: LCSH: Yang, Ke, 1957—Translations into English.
 Classification: LCC PL2922.K6 A2 2017 | DDC 895.11/52—dc23
 LC record available at https://lccn.loc.gov/2017003538

The paper in this book meets the guidelines for permanence and durability of the Committee
on Production Guidelines for Book Longevity of the Council on Library Resources, Inc. ∞

1 2 3 4 5 6 7 8 9 10

CONTENTS

FOREWORD

While Yang Ke has been an important poet for well more than three decades, he first burst onto the national Chinese poetry scene as the editor of the hugely influential 1998 *Yearbook of China's New Poetry*, which included nearly one hundred poets and essays by more than a dozen poetry critics and presented a distinctly southern Chinese voice to a national Chinese poetry scene that was still largely dominated by Beijing. The volume's preface was the now-famous essay "The Light of Poetry, Cutting through the Chinese Language," written by another southwestern Chinese poet, Yu Jian. Together, Yang Ke and Yu Jian set a powerful, if polemical, tone for Chinese poetry at the turn of the millennium. In many ways, Yang Ke's editorial poetics helped give shape to a now-aging division that still frames poetry discourse in China decades later. On one side is the term "intellectual," which has a negative connotation associated with cultural elitism and refined language, on the one hand, and with formal experimentation and poetic difficulty, on the other; and in the Chinese context, it also connects these elements to Western influences thought to neglect the "live scene" of Chinese society. On the other side is the term "popular," which thus refers to a myriad of oppositional positions that embrace vernacular language and common-lived and working-class experiences and themes, but it also implies a shift to more China-specific poetics.

As we explore the impact of Yang Ke's editorial poetics, however, it is important to see that the long arch of his work complicates any simple binary of "popular vs. intellectual." In 1989 he was appointed the poetry editor of the Guangdong Writers Association's journal *Zuopin* (Literary works), and in 1998 he edited *Them: A Ten-Year Anthology* (from Lijiang Press), featuring works from the avant-garde journal *Tamen*. From 1998 through 2014 he edited the *Yearbook of China's New Poetry* (Jiangsu Art and Literature Press), which is akin to America's *The Best American Poetry* anthologies. He has also edited *Outstanding Poems of the Nineties* (Lijiang Press, 1999), as well *Sixty Years of Chinese Poetry for Young People* (China Youth Press, 2009) and the *Misty Poetry Anthology* (China Youth Press, 2009). Like all editors, he has been both praised and vilified for his selections each year, but he remains an important force in discovering and championing new poetic voices over the decades.

While one must acknowledge Yang Ke's influential editorial contributions to Chinese poetry and poetics since the late 1990s, it is equally important that his editorial vision not overshadow the fact that he himself has remained a vital part of the Chinese poetry community for well more than three decades. In 1985 he won the top poetry prize in his home province of Guangxi. In 1987 he was selected for the "Young Poets Gathering" by the national journal *Shikan* (Poetry journal), widely considered the most prestigious in China. Since 1985 he has published eleven collections of poetry, including *Yang Ke's Poems*, released in 2015 by one of the most famous publishing houses in China, the People's Literature Press. He has also published three collections of essays. His poems can be found in numerous anthologies, including the *China's New Literature Series* (1976–2000), the *Centennial Collection of China's New Poetry*, and *University Language and Literature*. While *Two Halves of the World Apple* is Yang Ke's first full collection to appear in English, his work has been published and read widely outside China, and translated into Japanese, German, French, Korean, and Indonesian, as well as English. His awards include the prestigious Lu Xun Literature Prize for Guangdong Province and the Chinese Contemporary Poetry Distinguished Achievement Award (2000–2010), the competition for which was conducted by popular vote on the Internet.

As we turn our attention to Yang Ke's poetry itself, we often find in his early work an element of incantation, which is clearly tied closely to his proximity to minority peoples in South China. He frequently shifts registers and activates aspects of Chineseness that are often deemed marginal or peripheral to mainstream cultural themes and voices. For instance, in his poem "Walking toward Flower Mountain," we find oral textures associated with Zhuang minority folk idioms:

1.

Hey-yo hey-yo—
I am a paean in blood   I am a tribute to fire
From the tip of a boar's tusk I came
From a pheasant's fluffed-up feathers I came
From strange power of bone ornaments I came
Having snuffed out the ravenous glow in a wolf's eyes I came
Having faced down the flaming stripes on a tiger's brow I came
From a straight arrow and a stout bow I came here
Stepping over death agonies of my prey
Hey-yo blood   *hey-yo* fire
Hey-yo fierce beauty
With sword raised   beating a drum   to a gong's beat I came
—Ni-lo!

In many of Yang Ke's poems, readers will find themselves moving through layers of ethnographic details associated with the Zhuang minority culture or with other ethnic groups, ancient and modern alike. The notes added by translator Denis Mair, like the poems themselves, help locate the reader within the particulars of the landscape. "Totem," for instance, includes six translator's notes to help unpack the dense layering of culturally specific details— letting us know that the town of Willow River (Liujiang) is near the sacred mountain of Emei shan in Sichuan, for example, and that it preserves Song-era buildings; and that Zhenpiyan is a Neolithic site just south of Guilin City, first excavated in 1973, and the descendants of its original inhabitants retain their forest-dwelling culture today in the remote mountains of Guangxi and Vietnam and avoid contact with outsiders. For both the poet and his translator, poems become apertures through which we travel to learn and ultimately expand our knowledge of the world both near and far in space and time. The poetics of this earlier period of Yang Ke's work suggest a desire to decenter mainstream concepts of what poetry is by including its disenfranchised, marginalized, or excluded "others" in a way that reminds one of Robert Duncan's notion of a "symposium of the whole" as reimagined by Jerome Rothenberg, who used this idea to frame the radical inclusivity of ethnopoetics: "all the old excluded orders must be included," Duncan wrote. "The female, the proletariat, the foreign; the animal and vegetative; the unconscious and the unknown; the criminal and failure—all that has been outcast and vagabond must return to be admitted in the creation of what we consider we are."[*]

In the Chinese context, one is more likely to associate these ethnographic impulses with the roots-seeking literature produced by Han writers during and after the "rustication" regimes that granted young, educated Han poets unparalleled access to local cultures and life-worlds, stimulating an expansion of what Chineseness might look like, especially in a post–Cultural Revolution context. Needless to say, this historical context is quite distinct from that found in the American context of ethnopoetics, which came under increasing critical pressure from the very groups it hoped to introduce into the poetic mainstream and canon. The politics of Yang Ke's ethnopoetic work and that of other Han writers who invoke ethnic minority and nondominant, local Han cultural forms have not, therefore, received the same kind of scrutiny in China as, say, the inclusion of multicultural materials in Anglo-American poetry in the United States, for instance, since Han Chinese poetry after the 1970s did not coincide with robust artistic and literary movements like the Black Arts Movement, the American Indian Movement, and the Asian American Movement, all of which pushed back against acts of appropriation by their largely white, often (though by no means exclusively) male contemporaries.

As the decades progressed, however, we find that Yang Ke's work responded to the dramatic changes in China as a whole, to the radical urbanization felt earlier and more strikingly in the special economic zones of southern China. Here in these dynamic, often tumultuous spaces, migrant workers transformed the urban landscapes where he would later focus much of his poetic energy, as we see in his poem "Chinese People":

Those migrant workers who have to demand their wages.
148 pairs of battered hands
held out from Daqing's caved-in mine.
Li Aiye, who contracted AIDS after giving blood.
The shepherd bachelors of the loess slopes.
Gossipy women licking a finger to count money.

---

*Robert Duncan, "Rites of Participation" (1967), in *Symposium of the Whole: A Range of Discourse Toward an Ethnopoetics*, ed. Jerome Rothenberg and Diane Rothenberg (Berkeley: University of California Press, 1983), 328.

In poems such as "Nowadays High-Rises Are the Crops of the City," Yang Ke portrays the changing Chinese landscape as one where rice paddies are drained to create high-rise landscapes, while also describing how these changing landscapes affect the people who live there:

> Those who face gentrification watch over ancestral paddies
> A high wind is blowing in the sky as the economy slumps
> Large-scale developers shout their misery to the heavens
> All day with tireless zeal they keep tilling this field of new hope

In the poem "Railway Station," he furthers this theme when he writes:

> Here the stomach of the metropolis absorbs the new and purges the old
> The plaza is its huge ulcer, its exit is like a drainpipe
> Expelling a mixture of fish and dragons
> So many of them plain, decent folks   unassuming like grains of rice
> The noon hour resounds with a clash of twelve dialects

This ethically invested poet is the Yang Ke most have come to know—the poet who writes through the experience of those under the feet of globalization's unyielding march. Still, it would be shortsighted to limit our view of Yang Ke to the live-scene poetics of the popular school. He must also be read as a member of what is known as China's "Third Generation," alongside the likes of Han Dong and Zhai Yongming and others whose work appeared after the 1980s Misty Poetry generation, which included such major poets as Bei Dao, Duo Duo, Gu Cheng, and Mang Ke. As is visible in this collection of works written over a period of thirty years, Yang Ke's poetry engages with China's changing social realities, but he has always written with a densely lyrical line, full of natural landscapes and other strikingly beautiful imagery. So while some of his most well-known critics and commentators might want to keep him pigeonholed into the "popular" school, others have acknowledged that his poetry has always maintained a delicate balance of form and content.

One of the most striking things about this poet is that for Yang Ke, poetry is so much more than the writing on a page. For him, poetry is something we do in community, something that is best when engaged in together. In this sense, his life and his work as an advocate for poetry in all its forms is something of a poem in itself. And perhaps one of his greatest poems will be written by the younger generations of poets he continues to support and champion: Yang Ke organizes the Children's Poetry Festival in Guangdong Province every year, where he invites famous poets to judge poems by 200,000 contestants, and he continually tours schools to meet with students, whom he encourages to read and write more poetry. Taken as a whole, Yang Ke the editor, the organizer, and the poet reveals something profound about the permeability of each role, how each infuses the other, and how poetry is as much a social practice as the poems we leave behind.

JONATHAN STALLING

TWO HALVES OF THE WORLD APPLE

WALKING TOWARD FLOWER MOUNTAIN (SUITE)

Flower Mountain (Huashan) is located in Ningming County, Guangxi Province, along Mingjiang River. Around fifteen hundred rough-edged human figures are painted on a cliff face in cinnabar, bursting with raw vitality. The largest of the figures is 3 meters tall, and the shortest is around 30 centimeters. The figures are spread over an area 40–50 meters high by 170–180 meters wide. This spot is widely thought to be the cultural fountainhead of the Zhuang minority.

1.

Hey-yo hey-yo—
I am a paean in blood   I am a tribute to fire
From the tip of a boar's tusk I came
From a pheasant's fluffed-up feathers I came
From strange power of bone ornaments I came
Having snuffed out the ravenous glow in a wolf's eyes I came
Having faced down the flaming stripes on a tiger's brow I came
From a straight arrow and a stout bow I came here
Stepping over death agonies of my prey
Hey-yo blood   *hey-yo* fire
Hey-yo fierce beauty
With sword raised   beating a drum   to a gong's beat I came
—Ni-lo!
. . .
From nodding ears of millet I came
From corn tassels lit up by sunlight I came
From ravines and garden strips no wider than a conical hat
To the whiz of a full-swung machete blade I came
By power of flames to clear planting grounds I came
Hey-yo blood   *hey-yo* fire
Hey-yo for ripe, bursting beauty
With joyful songs   hopping like sparrows   we come dancing
A bride tosses an embroidered ball behind us
Red-dyed eggs smacked shell-to-shell as we come
Barn-houses of spotted and yellow bamboo rise at our heels
We carefully press rice cakes in family molds
Steam from our five kinds of rice wafts downwind
We are a paean in blood   We are a tribute to fire
Hey-yo blood   *hey-yo* fire
Hey-yo for beauty of exalted things

2.

A series of arrowheads aimed at the blood-red sun   loosed
At a wild bull with eyes as red as the sun
A mountain man of Luoyue clad in rawhide
Bellows straight from his rawhide-clad soul
His bellow is like that of a red-eyed fighting bull
Sounds of his own footsteps cheer him on
All across the wild slopes . . . he steps over
Moans of companions fallen in bamboo thickets
The might of his arm
Drives the shaft of his spear
Straight into a leopard's mouth

The cliff seethes with raging blood
Wind whips past the forest trees
Past the heart's flapping banner

Luscious smells of evening
Hang over a hearth fire
Snapping of green firewood
Shoots up sparks to join stars in the sky
Sending up tales of Old Buloto, who fought the Thunder King
And of Mother Le's visit to heaven
And dreams of a feathered man

The embers long ago died down
Now only this timeless message
Still blazes across the cliff face
More primitive than pictographic signs
More sacred than the sun

3.

Even the wind was massacred
Gutted heath   the final resting place
Of skulls that kissed the sword   blood that drenched arrows
Corpses puddled in blood
Hoof-pounding melee now recumbent
Clanging massacre   blades hacking flesh
Outright cruelty or cold torture
Rising crescendo of war gongs
Summoning bows and swords   summoning rattan shields
Not despairing even when mothers wail
From ruins of established tribes
Youthful stockades sprang up
By way of more deaths   barbarity led the way to civilization
Oh the maiden who sounded a drum with her severed arm
Was passed down in folk songs
Worshipped as the heroine of her people

Although cooking smoke was severed by sharp blades
Some found a riverbank where it could grow lushly
A marsh once soaked in blood
Cast off the heroic era of brass drums
Yet never once did war turn rusty
Blood in grim and vivid hues
Sinful and holy, washed over the land

Through wind-whipped waves   past sails torn to pieces
Step into a junk that hoists no sail
Track the bear wounded by an arrow   its trickle of blood
Run toward the hunter who wears a quiver
Turn toward offerings of netted fish
Turn toward offerings flushed from thickets
Beauty of nakedness   of yielding warmth

Pent-up blood dissipates in time   whitecaps sweep away loneliness
From loftiest peaks   torrents of love race down
Horns of tempting dilemmas fade away in time
Young hearts were ignited by an embroidered ball

1984

Translated by Denis Mair

FLOWING FIRE IN THE DEEP VALLEY

Redwater River
    comes
    walking
    out
From rocks
Big big kapok flowers
Gently burn
Mountain crags
In bronze sunshine
Congeal around a valley
    red birds
    bloody waves
    mountaineers like stolid rocks
Light bounces from bare backs
A coppery hue melding with land and sky

(Are the bleats of goats also red?)

Myths of beastliness   myths of the backcountry   myths of release
From headwaters flowing ever farther, drift of noisy days
Hurriedly they come
    floating
    down

Wind of the male beast
Roars out its commanding passion
O this water can burn
Fire in whorls
    inebriate
inebriate
In whirlpools

Redwater River
Blood vessel of mountains
Overflowing with flames

1985
Translated by Chao, revised by Denis Mair

GREAT MIGRATION

> In order to construct a terraced series of ten hydropower stations
> according to plan, 240,000 inhabitants were relocated.
> —*Redwater River Planning Report**

Raise—it—overhead

Carry that urn of fragrant wine overhead
Raise those sealed-off seasons above shoulder height
With trembling arms
Swaying to gasping breaths like a mountain beech
Oh waterfall of wine
It tilts
Spills
That reddish-brown flame with such enlivening power
Gives way to a suffocating blueness
Now a hearthstone's column of smoke   rises apart from others

In pieces now   that rugged old urn shaped by quiet toil

There is a white-colored farewell[†]
Streamers flapping on the trail
From high on the mountain
Pouring down
Into the valley
Rising and falling like waves
Wordless and subdued—the whole village's gaze
The whole village watches, subdued and wordless
Set loose at a creeping pace
A gravestone as silent as a cliff face
Now an unvisited island
The love story of troll and naiad becomes possible

Crow of rooster, bark of dog, moo of cow, shout of woman, tang of fish, reek of goat, smell of sweat, fragrance of rice
Scatter like mist

Uuwww ...
Off toward the sun and higher ridges, to the crashing of gongs
History of squatting burial, of tattoos and shorn-headed vows
Forever left behind on the cliffs, forever
Descendants of Buloto†
Following the course of the Redwater River
In the direction
Of a requiem
They go forward

1985
Translated by Denis Mair

---

* The Redwater River (Hongshui He) is a tributary feeding into the Pearl River from the west. It runs
  through the mountains of Guilin and the Zhuang minority area of Guangxi.

† According to the beliefs of many Chinese minority groups, the road after death that leads to limbo or the
  afterlife is white. White is thus the color of mourning.

‡ Buloto was the legendary progenitor of the Zhuang minority.

LITTLE SILVER CHILD

Black hill
White fog
(*Oh* fog . . . *Oh* fog . . . *Oh* he was singing)

White goats vanishing
White berries vanishing
A fogbank soon to drop its lamb
Drifts toward us from porcelain white hills
The whole world is bleating

Is the wooliness of a sheep like fog?
Does the fog have a sheep's blank whiteness?
He was calling: *Oh* fog . . . *Oh* fog . . . *Oh* fog . . .
He was tired
And cold
Seated on a slate-blue rock
Warming himself at a fire

More heavily than a stone he slept
Oh fog   *Oh* fog   *Oh* fog . . . *Oh*
From crystalline rocks calcined by fire
Slate-blue stones melted by fire
Down poured a river of tin
        A river of antimony
        A river of mercury

A silvery river of metal
And he became a silver child
Oh fog . . . *Oh* fog . . . *Oh* fog
Haunting wild hills and hollows
Heard by those who dug the shafts
And those who worked the mines
In slate-blue rocks he sang
In crystalline rocks he sang
Oh fog . . . *Oh* fog . . . *Oh* fog

1985
Translated by Chao, revised by Denis Mair

TOTEM

That day in the museum you called to me in a whisper
I suddenly realized the name being called was mine
With my strange high cheekbones, bridgeless nose, and jutting chin   I am one of the Willow River People*
    catching blind fish in White Lotus Grotto
I am one of the Zhenpiyan people, buried squatting ten thousand years ago and now transformed into a fossil†
The hidden tattoos on my skin resemble printed fabrics of the Zhuang, Tong, and Miao peoples
Memories of my artistry remain only on print blocks of red and gray clay
With the sun hanging from my left ear and the moon from my right, I rest in a cliff-hanging coffin that lets my soul ascend
I am bound on a course to the eternal, the infinite, and the remote
I am a father who sits wrapped in blankets on the birthing couch as the "childbearing male"‡
I am a woman committed to matrilocal ties who brings her husband to live with her
When jujube flowers wither and haws shrivel and even the stars drop
I am surely the one who sits on a bluff, year after year, singing courtship songs

The one who awaits a bygone year is me
The one who remembers a future day is me

Last year in Los Angeles I heard you whoop in the crowd
I suddenly realized that young bodybuilder who dead-lifted China's pride to the sky was none other than I
I'm a starry-eyed youth dreaming of a feathered man as I walk out of the Aeronautical Institute
I'm the one who presents a paper on futurology, then goes out to dance at a discotheque
I'm the red figure who jumped straight from a Flower Mountain rock face onto the Zhou brothers' canvases
Having passed through battle smoke at Jintian and raining bullets at You River§
I am the one from whose flag a bullet hole stares forever
I am the grinning bird perched on an Indian olive tree imitating Third-Sister Liu's folk songs‖
I am the Lijiang boatman who can deal with customers in English, Japanese, Cantonese, and Mandarin#
Big rivers have changed course, mountain streams have changed course, even rainy winds have changed course
I must be the Redwater River, which has run from deep in the mountains, red-tinted and steady, for ever so long

I am the one who awaits a bygone reality
I am the one who clearly remembers our future history

That day on the street, seeing your face and his face amid the crowd of faces
Damn it   I suddenly knew: I am you and you are he and he is none other than I!

1985
Translated by Denis Mair

---

* Willow River (Liujiang) is an old riverside town near Emei Mountain in Sichuan that preserves Song-era buildings.

† A Neolithic site at Zhenpiyan, south of Guilin City, was first excavated in 1973 and was found to contain graves and stone implements dating back almost ten thousand years. The ethnic resettlement program of Guangxi Province has identified approximately a thousand primitive forest dwellers who are thought to be descendants of that culture. These surviving Zhenpiyan people are scattered in remote mountains in Guangxi and Vietnam, avoiding contact with outsiders. Their relation with other minority groups in Guangxi is not clearly understood.

‡ Up until modern times, there was a curious custom among the Zhuang people. The father of a newborn baby would rest during the lying-in period, and would even be cared for by the birth mother!

§ Jintian was a town in Guangxi Province where the Taiping rebels fought their first two battles against the Qing Dynasty army in 1850. You River was the area in Guangxi Province where General Kan Weiyong, after several victorious battles against the Japanese, finally died in battle in 1944.

‖ "Grinning bird" here refers to Lielie-niao, the name of an animal character in the children's musical *Go, Bird, Go!* (*Xiaoniao jiayou!*). *Third-Sister Liu* is the title of a movie (1960) and the name of a character played by Huang Wanqiu. The movie is set amidst the beautiful scenery of Guilin. Third-Sister Liu was a legendary songstress of Guangxi whose "mountain songs" roused the people to stand up against harsh rule by officials. The actress Huang Wanqiu went on to become deputy director of the Guilin City Cultural Affairs Office.

Lijiang is a Pearl River tributary flowing in from the west. It passes through Guangxi Province.

CONTEMPORARY POETRY READING

Now that disco is more disco-ish than ever
Guys and gals are becoming more like poets
Clean white tablecloths are just perfect
For wing feathers to alight upon
Strange birds "nestle" in cups . . . then up they fly
All ears are open to be stuffed with images
A young fellow goes up to the stage
Then nonchalantly proceeds to vomit
Vomits up things like shoes and grenades
While fat and thin fingers both begin to point
Saying this fellow is no Freud
Though maybe you could call him Siggie
Meanwhile, someplace 100 meters away
Vendors are gnawing on duck legs
They have vaguely heard of poetry
And of something in this world called "Clear Pure Music"*

1986

Translated by Chao, revised by Denis Mair

---

* "Qingping-yue" (literally "Clear Pure Music") was a tune to which poets wrote lyrics in the Song era. Later poets wrote lyrics in the same form without singing the tune. Eventually the melody was lost, but the metrical form persisted. Many Chinese poets wrote lyrics in this classical meter, including Nalan Xingde and Mao Zedong.

A CERTAIN STATE OF MIND

Bullet holes in helmets and camouflaged fatigues
Open their mouths for a chorus
Let love fill this world
Butterflies take a bite out of Chuang Tzu's dream
And land on Kandinsky's flowers
A dead eye overflows with tears
Red bats yellow bats beautify a twenty-year-old summer
And girls in June are doves
A kind father buys his beloved son toy handcuffs
And dimples design traps for life

To collect welfare funds for the handicapped
A charity holds a horrific boxing match
A tap dancer performing on red carpet
Prances to a country music beat

Artists disputing loneliness create a heated atmosphere

1987
Translated by Chao, revised by Denis Mair

A KITE

I imagine it must be hard to get so high
Happiness cannot be the sky flying itself
But spirit's answering leap, a satisfied desire
When small hands of human childhood
Reach out for the upper world
Feathers of humble paper grow
Surpassing the freedom of fish and birds
Searching with the eyes takes time
Before its bright white form
Appears against pure blue
Its numerous graceful swoops
In carefree, lyrical measures
Sing a festival, a commemoration

1987
Translated by Chao, revised by Denis Mair

ELECTRONIC GAME

Twenty cents buys a turn:
Peace is made to stoop in submission
A bull lowers its horns
Friendly eyes spew sparks
Igniting a forest fire on Xinganling Ridge
Five thousand years are put to death
Only broken walls remain of Han Border
Chu River becomes a shallow ditch*

The Iraq-Iran border is hardly enough
Nor is shooting a white swan at Yuyuan Pool†
A paper-thin screen has been erected
To satisfy endless desires
And allow for wastage and slaughter
Wait, a wriggling black spot remains unshot
It is a fly
Open fire and annihilate it!

1987
Translated by Chao, revised by Denis Mair

---

* "Chu River" and "Han Border" refer to territory fought over by rival claimants to imperial power
  following the fall of the Qin Dynasty (221–207 b.c.). Later the phrase "Chu River–Han Border" came
  to mean the center line on the Chinese chessboard. Only after crossing this line can "soldiers" move
  sideways.

† Yuyuan Pool is a manmade lake at the Old Summer Palace in Beijing.

FIELDS IN THE NORTH

Where birdcalls are lost in silence

Plummy sorghum kernels exude a motherly bounty
Incisive tips of every corn leaf droop
Pulse of my blood circulates
In the South outside my skin
To such remote places
In a distant grove   an apple falls
As soundless as a dewdrop

There my native ground is found
Calm and gentle like a lake beneath ice
And motionless twilight steeps
In an ancient well, wherein the silence
Knowing no bounds   enters into my bones
Life becomes and does not become this landscape
And thus remains a tranquil cocoon
Even if it drifts to other waters

The language of autumn is born in stillness

1987
Translated by Chao, revised by Denis Mair

LISTENING TO A BRASS BAND

That night the sun was bright
Golden bees hummed and hovered
Entered the recesses of my consciousness
From the other side of midnight
While beyond music   drizzle strolls in darkness
Declaring autumn coolness without end

It seems the audience sits on a shore
And that the belly of a sea is a cicada
Waves of faces crashing freely
Animated faces are as ruddy as blood oranges
And everyone senses the brilliance of life

While beyond music   drizzle strolls in darkness
A time little different from any other

1987

Translated by Chao, revised by Denis Mair

THE OTHER SHORE

In April I approach step by step
A tombstone younger than I am
Not clear whether my life erects that slab
Or the slab is my body that won't collapse
Between human beings
There always exists a certain mood
Not conveyable in language
Just standing face to face must be enough

Always there exists a quiet river
Hidden in the ample depths of earth
Breeding so many roots
That few feel its existence
Man too is shaped from handfuls of dust
And thus ordinary
Like the earth or rocks
Once split they possess all the sky and sea
I wonder why
I became a cloud
Floating about until this chosen day
To return earthward, changing
Into the original tear
That streams unceasingly

1987
Translated by Chao, revised by Denis Mair

PURE LAND

Day and night the sick ward is drained of color
No distinction clearly cut
Between death and life
Trifling steps that tread to pieces
Those crystalline moonbeams
The soul sneaks by like a season
And now a shower
Suddenly falls upon a dried riverbed
The world left further and further behind
And the coastline kept in sight
Are like someone else's story
Life as small as a shell
Abandoned on the dune

1988

Translated by Chao, revised by Denis Mair

CHILLED WHITE WINE

Slowly, punctually, a bracing fragrance
Deliquesces through our bodies
A feeling like a fantasy
And our sight swims hazy
An instant of contact
Moistens all things
Life doesn't offer
Many such moments: a deliverance
From daily pressures   all things begin to rise
In suspension around our heads
One's life-force like an animated fluid
Transparent and fragrant   within a glass
Yet blood that beats increasingly fast
Predicts a special danger
Forcing us to proceed with caution
Lest the glass
Shatter ever so casually

1989
Translated by Chao, revised by Denis Mair

THE FOURTEENTH DAY OF SEVENTH MONTH

The Fourteenth Day of Seventh Month is a day for killing ducks
You and I and many others
Are willing to believe that ducks' souls are immortal
A river runs between the realms of sun and shade
Across which they swim, pure and white
To arrive on an eternal, pristine shore
People who reach it are reluctant to leave
Unlike those of us who scurry through this world
Only when we kill ducks
Will people over there come paddling across
To talk with us at night
Just now one of my feet, already in the river
Is sensing the gentle water
As life leaks between my fingers
I am reluctant to paddle
Though loneliness is palpable
And this world of suffering
Has no lack of memories bright and gloomy
Touching me to the core

1989
Translated by Chao, revised by Denis Mair

THE OLD HOUSE

Multicolored parrots fly to and fro in their cage
Repeat whatever they have heard
The door wears a solemn mask
And deep within
A darkness under the sun
Dragon-carved pillars
Weathered and in places refurbished
Patiently show: Time
Two clouds in black are weeping in the distance
And the weather forecast says thunder and showers
The world outside is fabulous
And the floor painted a thousand times
Can never be a blue sky

1989
Translated by Chao, revised by Denis Mair

SUMMER TIME CHANGE

Ahead of time, trains depart
Girls mature
Ahead of time, candles are blown out
That adorn their birthday cakes
And in a well-plotted murder
A knife goes in white
And comes out red
Ahead of time

Yet chicks refuse to crack their shell
The moon fails to light the sky
At nightfall

Yet a realist writer jogging in the morning street
Has been killed by the first bus
Which was running off schedule
So black humor and the absurdist school
Can at last be understood

And the guy headed for a date in the old place
At the old time has met another girl
The deceased—having just been cremated—
Has the wrong time listed on his certificate
And men stand bewildered over the theft
Of an hour of sun and air
Is time fair?

1989
Translated by Chao, revised by Denis Mair

THE SUNFLOWER

Here Van Gogh is buried
Every inch glorious
An imperishable grave
The brilliance shining to the fullest
Comes from his soul
And pierces all the days and nights
Making artists who follow
Unable to open their eyes

Yet when he was alive
An age was blind
Only after his death
Did friends and lovers
Seek him

Listening
To the internal monologue
Of a burning life

1989
Translated by Chao, revised by Denis Mair

WAYS OF OBSERVING THE RIVER

The river's arteries open
Tender as ever, its water
Calm or roaring
However it flows
Never torn from its banks
Its soil and its rocks

Banks exist beyond banks
As mountains beyond mountains
Careful to appear unfazed
Women have the river at their door
Men drift with the current as well
Yet in the human spirit
Lies the essence of water
Invulnerable in its utter softness

1989
Translated by Chao, revised by Denis Mair

BAMBOO

Draw out bones from my body
Plant them in the soil
They will grow a bamboo grove
Supporting my patch of home ground
And in their graceful sway
The whole world will be a landscape

Strips of bamboo dancing before the blade
Sharper than the blade
Bamboo-ribbed concrete   gripping crushed rock
Is deeply implanted in my language and poetry
My pulse synchronized with nodes of bamboo
Conversant with the spirit of the earth and sky
Hence charged with resonant energy
My life presents a natural green color

Though poor, seeing these shapes of bamboo
Each day, I am substantially satisfied

1990
Translated by Chao, revised by Denis Mair

NOBILITY

At the edge of night outside the balcony
A devious scheme is unfolding
As I write alone, a golden bell is struck and rings
The way between lines is bright and clean

Faces of masters appear behind words
We contemplate each other for a while
And I sense a mysterious attraction
Some kind of silent strength like religion
Leading me to break through the siege
Of darkness
And I am spiritually noble and pure
Drawing near the open sky of human nature
From a bird's-eye view   suffering is insignificant
Past snowy mountains a black horse gallops
Its beauty rouses the heart

Language and harvest each give life to the other
Grow vehemently in the spring of winters
I am caught up within them, my life awakening
Once more it shines, surviving countless disasters
Sonorously the golden bell is ringing

1990
Translated by Chao, revised by Denis Mair

RAILWAY STATION

Here the stomach of the metropolis absorbs the new and purges the old
The plaza is its huge ulcer, its exit is like a drainpipe
Expelling a mixture of fish and dragons
So many of them plain, decent folks   unassuming like grains of rice
The noon hour resounds with a clash of twelve dialects
Twelve interlopers lose their sense of direction at the same time
A sheepherder who wants to get rich   walked and rode from far north
Jostling with everyone else   he begins to taste the loneliness of crowds

Faux-diamond glare of a signboard flashes its fairy tales
That sexy lady on the billboard—does she get homesick?
Stray gusts of wind   chase streams of people off in all directions
Among them, cops and robbers never tire of playing hide-and-seek

Noise and exhaust smoke blanket the space within the iron fence
Along any level block, hidden pitfalls could be waiting
Each day, skirmishes to gain vantage points break out
Even sparrows on the corner are easily startled

Dreams in reinforced concrete radiate in all directions
Only this place that growth forgot is looking worse for wear
Major arteries radiate to distant spots from here
A stunted heart is suspended—set apart at the center

1990
Translated by Denis Mair

NELSON MANDELA

An African lion has stepped out of the cage
The sun shines on a most South African face
In a moment he brightens
And I see his soul
Like a black flame

Never brought to his knees
A man who survived
A million years of suffering
The dignity in his bones lent beauty
To the world's deepest skin color
Freedom-planting bird, even in his cage
Never separated from wings and wind

Truth glows like his smile
Nelson Mandela steps out of the prison

February 11, 1990
Translated by Chao, revised by Denis Mair

LISTENING TO A SERENADE BY MOZART

Like the queen-of-night flower that opens its petals nocturnally

Mozart, you are music
A century plant that sways with melody
Transparent tongues
Having savored the dark taste of death
Tenderly lick the wounds of my life

I cannot enter your soul
Just as I cannot overleap a rainy season
To reach the sun
Yet truly I can touch your voice
And sense your pure cleansed notes
Seeds of light in the night
Making decorative lamps look unreal

March 20, 1990
Translated by Chao, revised by Denis Mair

IMAGINING WEST HUNAN

Days of bad weather
In the city, a dull atmosphere

I can't go out
So, alone I read a novel dated 1934
And imagine West Hunan
The towns of springtime by the border there
Crystalline puddles
Like lamps on flagstones

Imagine a maiden floating   out of a song in a dream
Her scent like mint
I begin to harbor a gentle feeling
Inexplicable like you, Master
Beauty can't help but be heart-rending
Our intimacy under the moon
Like peach petals in threes or twos
Falling in a clear stream
Showing what is gone is gone forever
Imagining West Hunan
And I am reluctant to go out visiting
For those peepholes growing on city people's doors
Look open yet are blinder than the blind

Imagining West Hunan
Imagining that bright girl
Is enough to intoxicate me

March 24, 1990
Translated by Chao, revised by Denis Mair

GREAT WATER

> My life is inseparable from water, education, and writing.
>
> —Shen Congwen

In you, Sir, I perceive an elusive taste like water
Like a hot spring in a wild, remote place
Like quiet drizzle in the wind   moistening the roots of living things
Or a single dewdrop holding its roundness
On snowy petals of Tao Qian's chrysanthemum hedge

Like a deserted slope after new rain   what rain could be newer?
Elusive beyond flavor   hinting at the taste within taste
Bright and clear for a lifetime
Longjing tea in celadon   a sea of pale green steeping
Cracked glaze of the pour-off bowl   holding the eye with its finish
A pattern of pellucid ripples
Banquet liquor fermented with special water   yielding more savor with the years
Kept underground   within our bodies
Where it burns slowly

April 13, 1990
Translated by Denis Mair

REREADING *FORTRESS BESIEGED*

—for the author Qian Zhongshu

You in the city were in fact
Helpless
You once charged toward an invisible wall
As if pricking the sky with a bamboo pole
So you put on a mask of nonchalance
Befuddlement does not come easy

A great bell that does not ring when it is struck
The greatest wisdom is like ignorance
And the curtain hanging closed
Takes on the deepness of the sea

Rereading *Fortress Besieged*
I understand, Master, that you pondered
And found earnestness to be a mistake

April 21, 1990
Translated by Chao, revised by Denis Mair

HOT SPRING

Slip into the water   listen intently
Soft plashing of spring water
Touches you right to the marrow
Enveloping warmth
Between skin and naked skin   coaxing fatigue
To ascend   as water's warmth
With its insistent teeth   causes enmity
To melt away gradually
Water caresses me and enfolds me
I sense ageless feelings that were suppressed
Can frigid air freeze a hot spring solid?
Can rock strata obstruct a hot spring?
Love has materiality   a thermal current
Emerging from thousands of meters underground
From remote darkness
In deep places of history

Bathing in water at a constant temperature
My body and my soul
Are as pristine as at their origin

April 30, 1990
Translated by Denis Mair

TERRA-COTTA WARRIORS

For the supreme glory of a dead man
A mighty array of soldiers in thirty-eight columns
Is plunged into ever-repeating night   a battle cloaked in darkness

Years blacker than a grave   bitterness deeper than the deepest sleep
Buried figures of officers, kneeling archers, horsemen
Laying waste to all within a hundred miles
Your expressions are blank
Following orders is a soldier's highest calling
In victory you don't carouse   yet you drink blood as wine
Not deigning to look at corpses strewn across the heath
Your wide-open eyes staring blindly
Barbarically imposing an inane discipline, absurd order
Figures of men in armored tunics, standing archers, generals
Summon you to the ultimate collection of despotic burial relics

From now on you will know no daytime
Your sun was the First Qin Emperor, and he has fallen
The long night drags on   halberd blades are your cold crescent moons
Holes pierced by arrowheads are your lightless stars
Figures kneeling, riding, giving orders
Your precipitation isn't rain   daybreak brings no light
Oblivious to firecrackers on New Year's, joss smoke at Mid-Seventh Month
Horses' manes need wind to stir them   grand gales cannot enter death's city
For such as you there is no chance to dandle children on your knee
You don't even recall that there are flowers and women's lips in the world
The years are blacker than the grave   this bitterness deeper than the deepest sleep

Yet your fortitude is imposing, even as you buckle
Standing erect is in itself a miracle
Your skulls are hollow   your legs are sturdy
Six-foot bodies still upright   a grove of timeless plaques
You were sacrificed to slavish loyalty
Yet you embody the strong intellect of a culture
Figures of men in armored tunics, standing archers, generals
You perform an enduring tragedy   enact a grand statement
The coffin lid of the man you guard has long since been closed
His merits and crimes were weighed in the balance
Yet time has rendered no final judgment
Woe is me   the time has come to depart, my soul!
Away from this well that can yield no water*

June 22, 1990
Translated by Denis Mair

---

* The terra-cotta warrior pit was discovered in 1977 by a farmer digging a well. The figures were sculpted to serve as a subterranean army in front of the First Qin Emperor's tomb.

EVENING SYMPHONY, GUANGZHOU, 1992

The brilliant beauty of material things
Burns day and night in the city's chest cavity   upon its back

And in the canyon of high-rise buildings
The music that flees
Like a sleepwalker's meanderings
Is a distillation of beauty   purified
By the pure love that refuses to flood its banks
Is human religion, eternal and absolute

Soft petals   petals stripped of all wealth
Fill hollows in the uncrowned capital of merchandise

In a soaring widespread intoxication
Man is freed from material bondage
Approaching the ultimate with perfect, noble steps
Upward to the sky   walking on piano keys

1992
Translated by Chao, revised by Denis Mair

FASHION MODELS

Staring at an ad, bedazzled
A leopard stalks my field of view
Graceful, glamorous
Only eternal simplicity is lost

Odor of cloth, odor of makeup and of leather
Happiness found in hidden satisfaction
One senses a great hand
Is pushing History, changing
Our stubborn habits
Testament to merchandise and modern civilization
A man should be thankful in his life
For iron, oil, and the excellence of cement

Fragrance lurks, welling within
The rose of industry sparks my ardor
Yet I remain uncaptured

1992
Translated by Chao, revised by Denis Mair

IN THE CONDO RUSH, WISHING FOR A HOMELAND

"Home"—the very word root of humanity and my life
First warmth in womb
Cradle of dreams
Rice and fire   shelter and survival
A log that floats to you in a flood

The cocoon and nest to which
Even the furthest wayfarer looks for respite

Space we build, like birds and bees
With wood and soil
All through our life of toil

When the key is made of gold
The building monstrously tall
The moon of the twentieth century
Suspended above the window
"Home" gets lost in rows of condo towers

1992
Translated by Chao, revised by Denis Mair

1992, YEAR OF THE HORSE

1.

Blood in frenzy   desire-swelling flesh
Flight on the ground
Spiritual light   another kind of lightning
Four hooves that live for leaping
Ten grasslands reflected
In the horse's eyes

2.

Enthusiasm of drifting imagination
Pegasus dancing in clouds
Introspection of a solitary soul
Journeying the void
Ignoring things basic and trivial

3.

Hooves prance into a New Year
The echoing tread of Fate
Its breath may betide an unbroken rainbow

4.

War is a game for horses
Swords and murderers
Bloody entrails from a wooden horse
As for those on horseback
The more they kill, the more heroic

5.

From a wastrel who caught cold
We hear no whickering but his sneeze

6.

The deer was perforce called a horse
On the whim of a brute with a sword
Snakes danced
Subduing thousands of horses
Under the shadow of whips

Only subject to
A plant most delicate and fragile
The moonbeams in the eyes of a horse
Are like drops of dew
Resting on petals

7.

The drunken kingdom begins to run
Like a swallow in flight
A sensitive hoof
Can sense wings flapping

The horse—a state of being and a gesture of flight
Turns into bronze and boredom

8.

Creature of violent energy
Bets on speed
Riders in the race
Are not the real winners or losers

9.

A horse, the first passionate flower
Of life ready to burn and end
With blessings of bodily beauty
It will never shrink from sacrifice

1992
Translated by Chao, revised by Denis Mair

POETRY ETUDES

1.

The odor of a garden after rain
Exudes a breath of death
A piece of paper left smudged with black and red ink
Imps that danced naked scurry away
On the muddy road, tiny footprints
Wind blows remnant voices from tips of grass
Dimming redness of a branch's last bloom
Is like a beautiful widow

2.

The fire leaps in the stove
A fairy dances in embroidered shoes
Bright laughter   sends out waves of heat
Her hot tongue makes you rejoice
In absolute beauty
A rootless plant yields the loveliest blossoms
Blue butterflies fly dreamily away

3.

I touch the blood-red crown of dawn
A cock chants its high-pitched praise, bells toll on all sides
Peach blossoms petal by petal send forth spring's message
Joyous and delicate, like a newborn's cry
High buildings are torches blooming in the rain
Brilliance of Chinese words   flashes inside an urban village
From lantern to lantern, from waking to waking
Chicken feathers strewn about   as time slips by
A man walks on paper, sings in full voice
Yet silence resonates above all

1992
Translated by Chao, revised by Denis Mair

STROLLING AMID COMMODITIES

Strolling amid commodities, disquieted
Life itself is consumption
Human forms in movement
Reflected on glossy surfaces of objects
A tempest of feet   the background music of a great age
My mind aglow   rosy with good fortune
Senses stretching with pleasure
Silvery caress that touches the height of a city

A modern Eden, temple to the fetish
Of material goods   where my desires are consoled
Listening to the gospel, thankful for the gifts of life
My way the must-go way
Thereby I return to material things   to humanity's root
And re-enter life from another point of view
In awe and piety I pray
And crown a new century
Let it baptize my soul again   in a rain of gold

September 5, 1992
Translated by Chao, revised by Denis Mair

OIL

1.

liquid rock that structures modern civilization
the cold flame inside stone
a zero-degree passion, prolonged black sleep
sustained in time's abyss
two absolutely unmixable elements, fire and water
blend perfectly at the core of things
dark dormant horse
eternity's midnight blood, a wave that stops breathing
river of light no one can ford, galloping across heaven and earth
from one world to the next

2.

the death of oil is not the end of life
but a conversion, from hell into heaven
from one form into another
flame is intense prophecy
magnificent dreamlands are born in the brilliance of dying
no flowers are visible in the fire-blooming oil
the twentieth century: bright-blackest of fruits
endless unbroken sound, oil flows in chaos
its cycle of births and deaths is spectacular
infinite unlimited fumes
fill material space—even non-material space is inundated
plastic containers, petroleum jelly, synthetic fibers
oil gushes into all places where oil cannot be sensed
oil: the horse, the fuel, the cloth, the fountain of a new age
golden apples: dark and most glittering of all
today the movement of oil is human movement
and the history it writes is blacker than any ink

3.

like ripples in water, the damage is concealed
in a drop of oil, nature exhausts her resources
spirit collapsed, oil wells cannot quench the thirst in human hearts
surging, mobile—oil is impossible to define
in oil's unwavering gaze
the final green moment of consciousness is the most beautiful scene of all
spotless, unsullied moonlight, a clear beauty
irretrievable in the vehicle's rearview mirror

1993
Translated by Simon Patton

VALENTINE'S DAY CONCERT: EXTEMPORIZATION ON A THEME

It's a Valentine's Day concert   heart-shaped tickets flock through the door
Wing-to-wing   fleeting queen-of-night flowers take refuge from the darkness
Chinese folks, having lived for two thousand years within Lao Tzu's book
Painstakingly arrange an evening gala
It's an atmosphere of ambulatory roses putting on the ritz
Suits and evening gowns keep smiles on their faces
The program is arranged to give a privileged feel
Much like goblets of X.O bumping lightly together

Ancestors made do with plain fare   passed down observances
Focused on eating   serving *fish* at year's end*
For we eat auspicious homonyms   we eat ritual, culture, and self-lauding tales
We eat up all the leaves from mulberry trees that grow between fields
China has always been a giant hungry stomach   up until

Basic comforts are in place   then the mouth that found heaven in food
Is inflamed by desire   turns into a volcano mouth that immolates lovers
It becomes picky   wants a range of flavors
Chocolate, cola, Nescafé . . . as if making distinctions
Among consonants and vowel sounds
Blowing out candles that decorate a birthday cake
Letting roman letters cohabit with the mother tongue
In her ancient cave   spawning bastard terms like *tekshi* and *baibai*
Coining new words without the slightest consideration for old word roots

Ah, swirl of music in intimacy of turned-down lights
Soaring as if on wings of Kentucky Fried Chicken
In a sky fit for phoenixes   ardent and enchanting
A clangorous melody, whereby the city's soul
Impresses us with its pulsating brilliance

1993
Translated by Denis Mair

---

* The Chinese word *yu* 魚 (fish) is a homonym of *yu* 余, meaning abundance.

THIS IS THE LATEST ON YANG KE

He eats a pepper steak in a pub
then "grabs a cab," as they say in this town, then
wanders past stalls piled sky-high with color.
Here in the South, where night never falls
He watches money counterfeit love with female strangers—
His heart is half rotted away by now.
Once in a while   from a jumble of icily intelligent words known as poetry
he looks up
like a fly on its pile of rubbish.

1994

Translated by Simon Patton

GUANGZHOU

In China, for good fortune, please head to Guangzhou.

—proverb

From north to south, our People's Boulevard leads heavenward
A train's direction is the direction of fate
There is nameless eagerness on unpretentious faces
Showing the true countenance of my motherland

People meander across the station plaza
Squabbling like birds that strayed indoors
Worn out or not, who would shun this City of Flowers and Grain?
How I envy those dressed-up folks   fitting into conventional life
Like sunbeams enclosed between transparent panes of glass
Imagine the sound of a counting machine, riffling paper bills
This era's most marvelous music, and someone always gets to hear it
The desires of some people are always gorgeously fulfilled
Countless folks vanish along the way to Pearl Delta
Another cloudburst is absorbed into the soil
But some people are stuck in a prolonged delirium
They suffer straight from the beginning to the end
Once again their train's direction will be the direction of fate

February 23, 1994
Translated by Denis Mair

SELF-PORTRAIT, 1967

a happy sonofabitch* crossing the street
I was ten that year, had never ever seen a bare wall
green army uniforms made the summer exciting
I scampered in and out of the language of debate
learning how to read from political posters
my sensitive snout picking up the smell of burning
the sun was blistering that summer of raging slogans
a sonofabitch crossing through a revolutionary storm
classrooms empt-empt-empty
a sonofabitch crossing through a whiz of bullets
finally charging up onto the muzzle of a gun
more thrilled than I'd ever been, I had no idea what death was in my tenth summer
I felt like I was living in a movie
and had caught up with the life and times of the heroic Pavel Korchagin†
when I care-carefully picked up a bullet off the ground
what my fingers touched was only the start of the nightmare
in 1967 I saw faces vanishing into thin air with my own eyes
a jittery little sonofabitch crossing the street
and running as fast as it could from the scenes of 1967

March 7, 1994
Translated by Simon Patton

* The word *gouzaizi*, translated above as "sonofabitch," literally means "dog-spawn." During the Cultural
  Revolution (1966–1976), this term was used to refer to the children of parents classified as landlords,
  rich peasants, anti-revolutionaries, convicted prisoners, and so-called "Rightists" (intellectuals who had
  criticized the Chinese Communist Party).

† Pavel Korchagin is the worker-hero of the novel *How the Steel Was Tempered* by Nikolai Ostrovsky. The
  book was extremely popular in China (millions were sold) and was recently made into a television series.

A KAPOK TREE, BACKLIT AT SUNSET

Tree of dreams   as the expanse behind it sinks into twilight
Its backlit shape takes on a special clarity
There is a hint of swaying in its living upper limbs
For whom this loveliness   these eye-catching pastel lines?
Overflow of lingering beauty radiates into the air
Telling its tale of survival as far as light reaches
In this moment's cataclysm of the spirit
Enveloped in an aura of nobility
A tree toward which we lean admiringly
On the point of crawling in supplication

Whose hand is turning down the sun's lamp-wick?
Only its flames are still leaping
Blossom of desire   this season's invisible flower
Being blown toward high places by the final passion
My soul flies on the branch tips
As gloom closes in   all living things sink into it
In the scenery of the spirit
The silhouette one presents   means everything

November 30, 1994
Translated by Denis Mair

ON A DRIZZLY DAY, A TREE IN BLOOM

When it first enters my line of sight
It appears cleansed and groomed by rain
Drenched in a chilly wetness
Its naked black branches   show a touch of stiffness
As if wanting to scrape the sky

Not far off   a silent bridge over the Pearl River
Steep lines of girders
Hint at the city's rules

In a passing moment
I glimpse its other half of unclouded pastel
Rain-obscured flowers belonging to a private realm
By a trick of sight, the tree of blossoms comes forth to meet me
Yet I know a rooted tree cannot move
Wind sets the flowers tossing   an idle dance of flurrying thoughts

I've been through days that came down on me like landslides
I am too weary to sing of springtime
Warmth of blood was overcome by a chill in my bones
What a pushover I am, to be moved by what I felt just now
Remnant music at life's core   found its way to those flowers

March 14, 1995
Translated by Denis Mair

LIGHT OF THE SEA

Out of the ocean leap pieces of silver
Sparkling notes outrun snowy teeth of waves

The night's gale wakened a herd of horses   their backs are surging
Backs of crystalline horses dwindle amid distant whitecaps

A white virgin is swinging her braids about
As she traverses open ground   the surf makes folds in her robe

Limitless water   garrulous foam of words
History of speech melts away in rise and fall

Only light   by now only light grows in the abyss
Passionate churning   rays flung about like undulating fringe

A light-transfixed moment rouses death   the ocean feels a pang
Happiness reaches the parted hem of blue silk

Along a fault line in water   turbulence opens a salty wound
Irreclaimable remoteness   time reflected in a whirlpool's mirror

All sides lost in distant haze   beneath the watery wastes
Rest graveyards of human beings   villages of fish

Only light   only holy light in this world illumines tragedy
Whitecaps bloom over coral branches   mermaids   raise voices in song

Even the simplest coelenterates   also wriggle and void their wastes
Even the lowliest lives   create their own splendor

At the instant of each droplet's birth   its shape is inextinguishable
Radiant traits passed on in arcane ways   have power to dispel dustiness

Water is always interconnected   freedom in itself knows no boundaries
"It is the totality of all unbounded things"

"One who knows the inner marvels of light will embody the light"
"Illumined by inborn light from an eternal space"*

April 28, 1995
Translated by Denis Mair

---

* The three closing quotations are taken from Heidegger, Solzhenitsyn, and Eliot.

ROAD ON THE SEA

1.

Waves my eyes rest on have risen and fallen like this
For a million years   leaving whose footprints on the surface?
For a prow like an arrowhead   again and again the road
Fades in an instant   is born in an instant
Plunging by degrees   one sinks in depths of the self's shadow

More prolonged than a pendulum   more spacious than late autumn
Stretching farther than a grassland behind snowy peaks
Sailing routes intersect like countless gulls convening
Like a school of fish   scattering in all directions
The sea lies spread like fragments of quartz crystal
The sea   rent asunder   then always rejoining
Boats move across it like clothes irons
Creases of history are readily smoothed out

2.

A road is repeatedly peeled away from mud
Like a viable life leaving the womb   growing each day
Listen for its sound passing through clouds   emerging from water
A rainbow   in the air you smell the burn of friction
This road is outside of perception   where dreams cannot venture
A series of test wells dot the seabed   like a vein through your body
Like the feeler of an octopus
And none of this is simply imagination

3.

This road in liquid phase   continuous thread of beauty
This fluctuation full of passion and wetness and yielding warmth
The merest visual contact   connects to a boundless expanse
My body thrown open is a wonderful harbor   love floods in
Blueness replete and unrestrained   transparency holds color
What could be more holy than love and desire?
What could stretch further than a watery road?
"A sea that commits mistakes does not exist"*

This little village   this world that tears down barricades
Stones like waves stretch into the distance . . .

May 1995
Translated by Denis Mair

---

* Quoted from a poem by Odysseus Elytis.

A BUNDLE OF LETTERS

1.

"your voice comes, across distant time and space"
the left hand pressing the paper with heart-piercing force
facing, in an instant, many a thing that can't be recalled
such as the tone, the intonation, pauses organic and inorganic
even your heart murmurings, strong and weak
"the wholesome smells, and the body odors"
the instant pain, the person writing words, hidden in lined paper
of whom the character may let slip hearsay if not careful enough

putting the hand over the characters you wrote
the heaven-and-earth-sweeping feeling nearly striking one down
the characters so energetic, with enough force to wound and kill
"the hand over them could gain energy"
so much so that I seemed to be hovering over a face or something else
the most enticing part of it was to smell it, and you could taste the sun
"the gradated tones of an Oriental's skin have touching appeal"

that damned mosquito bit the arch of my foot
"isn't that as unbearable as licking someone's soul?"
by accident I swallowed a chrysanthemum
so smooth and slippery soft that one "sinks" in thought and "thought" sinks
thoughts emerged off and on, like gulps of muddy water
thirsty, then quenched, feeling so happy, but the throat gets stopped up with mud
thirsty and quenched again, life a bitter puzzle between head and body
at the instant of entering hell, despair comes welling up like first love
no one can really bear the "blows" of happiness
"what a luxury it would be to die in happiness"

2.

the south is an empty nest
and I am a lonely bird under the eaves, detached, cold
with a multiple personality, my wings used to embrace, not to fly
wind outside, occasional rain
peddlers and hawkers are sassing each other; women are blooming in their snail-shell homes
upon a husband's return to his pretty little woman, the master of the household
has changed
nietzsche is dead; smell it; it smells foul!
gauguin said what he wanted to establish was the right to do whatever he wanted

split a feather for me; I am turning vulgar, but no one cares
reading? writing? spending days fragmentarily like chickens and dogs
like mud at the bottom of the lake, feeling myself dying inch by inch
"how can you pass such a night alone if you are not writing?"

many people are not as good as a bird
really, what is up with these odd birds?

"don't listen to my rubbish! My mood is getting the better of me"
—just plain moody, and for no reason at all

3.
however, when I read your first letter
what you said taught my soul to fly

without your written words as evidence
the devil only knows who you are and what I'm doing
I do not know you but I am familiar with you, although I am in no position to prove your existence
I suspect the characters you wrote may have originated before the middle ages
the sneak attack of memory causes a dizzy sensation
at one's weakest it is easy to return to childhood
drawing a little water curtain closed, in a small space
one, two, three, four, five, six, seven . . .
making stroke after stroke, drooling, being serious
time turning the other way round, like a silkworm metamorphosing
you have two braids, long and thick; you look at people in a strange way
and I was your neighbor, "I'll call you big brother"
you always thought only you could call me that
crickets around the waist sang out a summer
entwined in wisteria, coiling and coiling some more

you made me feel pure, innocent
although I can't go back there again

sadness descends, mixed with unnamable desires
smoking a cigarette and imagining, again, a woman possessing all colors, scents, and tastes
who stood in front of Su Xiaoxiao's tomb like a renowned courtesan from some other era*
drawing gentlemen into encounters, sending them forth to conquer the world
acting demure, holding up one corner of her skirt, a free-wheeler if the truth be told†
for me such a person remains mysterious, not a threat
yet inexplicably devastating all before her

ah my, maybe neither of these fictions hits the mark
but it would be more unbearable for a man to stop imagining than for a woman
to stop looking in the mirror

4.

maybe my body was bound by your handwriting right from the beginning
its softness and tenacity lie not in the utterance, but in the impulse to entwine

I do not know who listens to the saint's words, who speaks unspeakably
in birdsong at dawn I hear a heart throbbing

through a budding flower I see part of you
you are physically real in my dream but nothing when I awake

I'm no longer moved by the melody of music or the rhythm of poetry
I'm moved only by "the signifier," moistened by lips and an open hand

burning. ascending. rosy clouds gathering, "kidnapped" by an angel
for a whole summer I have been vaulting and shimmering in your radiance

except that I am never sure whether this is an experienced event
or a desired illusion

5.

rubbish.
around me. around you.
—"so are you." "so am I."
we are being polluted. we accept it. and we say it's pretty good, happy

are we

separated by the sprawl of the objective world
busy, from one city to another
no real foundation, no real residence: status of the modern person.
status of human beings

an ant, always moving house but never seeing a home
a grain of rice on its forehead, picked up from no one knows where

"I suspect I am only sleepwalking"
and now you woke me up, made me feel I am alive
I—at present—here and now

like an inky thief that has vomited ink all day[‡]
its wrung-out gut now rinsed with water, its swollen form spread out
the longest tentacle reaching your chest, adhering to you

I feel that I should be somewhere else
I feel that I already am somewhere else

poetical fingers are peeling the "I" that is "yours" away from daily life
body and soul are in perfect sync, bursting with vitality
enveloped in invisible dense vapor that keeps out evil and shame
an atmosphere absorbing the atmosphere . . . an expanse of blue, an expanse of yellow

a flow of feeling, like pain after a tooth is pulled, faintly . . . .

since then we have looked down on happiness

6.

except that I am never sure whether this is an experienced event
or a desired illusion

July 24, 1995
Translated by Ouyang Yu

---

* Su Xiaoxiao was a famous Chinese courtesan in Southern Qi (479–502), whose tomb is found in Hangzhou near West Lake.

† *Fengliu* (literally "wind-flow") can mean dashing, gallant, fancy-free, breezy, or freewheeling.

‡ *Wuzei* (literally "inky thief") is the Chinese word for squid.

LITTLE ROOM

A little room is a magic box
Life that disappeared into a mirror
Reveals itself again

A great many concealed thoughts
The disheveled portion of a life
Which proliferates and spreads at night
Like a miasma from under damp straw
Upon returning to the room
Sunlight is kept out at the threshold
The fogged mirror shows human lassitude

Upon returning to the room
Soft-bodied animals
Probe with feelers into recesses
Hard plates of a carapace are slowly retracted
Releasing the beast
Within the body   reveling in the exchange of scents

But people walking outside make sure   they are seen as humans
Out on the avenue   they bask in wonderful sunshine
The huge greenhouse of sky   is everyone's ideal definition
Of their true room

February 26, 1996
Translated by Denis Mair

TELEPHONE • (ELECTRIC SPEECH)

1.

magnetic timbre, like a black eel swimming toward me out of the distance
invertebrate fish, electrified animal
wrapping around and around my nerves
you and I being invisible, who is there who can see?
under cover of emotion, we arrive at one other
a contact of voices seamlessly enmeshed
lip-petals, flowering and fading in a split second
narrow passageway, shaped like a cave
linguistic code entering ears. each of us
the compass direction and the exit so eagerly sought by the other
expression issues from this body
and disappears within the body of the addressed
teeth-lightning, submerged in the darkness of flesh

2.

telephone: freak of communication. a door
of conversation that can be opened at leisure
willful emasculation of space, cutting through language's metaphors
transporting us rapidly, whisking us into unusual stage sets
free movement of electric charge, conversion of acoustic frequency signals
discursive encounters: actually doubly reinforced wrong impressions
acute antagonisms composed by speaking and listening
narrative gaps vanish in the blink of an eye
it's not the conducting wire which conveys blockage—only a means of passage
between hearts a thousand knots from root to tip of the magic horn
two extremes of latitude and longitude   synchronized reactions and shocks of body and soul
without interruption, holographic signs become clear in the vagueness
like lizards darting in and out of clumps of grass
an ever-expanding auditory space growls with vitality
stranded in events of discourse and unable to extricate oneself
a nagging thirst for information and emotions

3.

nothing at all was "heard," nothing "said"
love is an endless sinking   transmission of warm currents
we open up the five senses completely and enter a state of frenzy
two-way transfer of both giddiness and smiles
no one is able to refuse contamination by another's saliva
when "self" and "other" are mutually encompassed
confession and attention coalesce
in the *hiss* of electric current, the soul creeps out of its shell
modern-day shaman of soul connection
a thumping heart can't help bursting into song

a brief phone call is a meeting for life

April 15, 1996
Translated by Simon Patton

---

* Here Yang Ke reworks lines from a love poem by the Tang Dynasty poet Li Shangyin (c. 813–c. 858). The relevant lines are "Last night's stars, last night's wind, / By the west wall of Painted Mansion, east of the Hall of Cassia. / For bodies no fluttering side by side of splendid phoenix wings, / Between hearts one minute thread from root to tip of the magic horn." According to the *Modern Chinese Dictionary*, "The rhinoceros was formerly believed to be a magical beast. Inside its horn there was a white line that ran from one end to the other." A rhinoceros horn thus alludes to an intimate understanding between two people (usually lovers). Note that Yang Ke replaces "thread" with "knots"—a kind of tangle that is both a connection and an obstacle.

MOTHER TERESA

—written upon hearing news of her death

This person who went among the crowd   this doer of charitable works
Begging bowl in hand   in a blue and white cotton sari
This spiritual seeker content with a lifetime of austerity
On a morning in Calcutta   stopped to rest her tired feet
She felt her strength ebbing away

For whom do the bells toll?   Strains of Diana's funeral choir
Have died down, not reaching where she rests in peace
An eminent figure under a lonely halo   set apart by holiness
Serving the poor meant she was no more remarkable than they
Fame was an unintended reward   "I am not worthy"

She saw herself as a pencil in God's hand
Miracles were traces of her patient, steady steps
Attending to tasks for those who had nowhere to turn
In an era of desire writ large, this was a kind of greatness
She was the Way, the Spirit, and the Truth

A lavish state funeral would have been superfluous
Her span of "living unto death" was already as plain as a shroud
Her diminutive frame grew frailer with the years, sleeping on a grass mat
She handed pills to lepers   washed clothes their swollen fingers could not hold
A poor woman who loved the poor   living authentically
Her eyes turned to low places   her soul ascended all the higher
As the gate of heaven opened, she kept looking back
Once again this maiden from Albania heeded
A summons from her inner heart to leave her home
"Go back to the earth, there are no slums here"

September 9, 1997
Translated by Denis Mair

PASSING THROUGH

At times the passenger sitting next to me
May be a girl dressed in a bustier or a denim skirt
Her physique like a bursting berry leaves me breathless
Silky fingers taper to polished nails
Tapping absent-mindedly on her purse
"Youth is beauty"
The sigh of a falling leaf is heard in my heart

I head from New Harbor Avenue toward Civic Conduct Street
The public bus just keeps trundling along
Steel gears push the conveyor belt of days
To and from work I follow my cyclical route
Passing through poetry to advertising copy   from Comrade to Mister

Right now the ones I'm rubbing shoulders with
Are two migrant workers in wrinkled clothes
Labels on their cuffs more conspicuous than spots on their shirt fronts
"Say, buddy, have you been earning anything?"
"Fat chance! I still need to get a short-term residence card
I haven't found a place that will vouch for me."
Their Sichuanese drawl betokens their fate
Of shuffling feet outside a Cantonese-speaking door

Motorcycles everywhere in the rearview mirror   of any status from unemployed to downsized
From Ocean Pearl Bridge to Ocean Impression Bridge
From vying to host the Olympic Games to the repatriation of Hong Kong
Overhead walkways look more and more weathered every day
Higher glass barriers are being built all the time
In congested space   inspiration is harder to come by than oxygen
The blue sky hung up in memory   by now is a stiffened towel
On a clothesline behind a construction workers' dorm

A clothing vendor boards the bus   her face glows with rosy possibilities
The mainspring of the city's alarm clock is wound up all the way
Her black dress shows a peek of cleavage   her perky breasts are unabashed
Like the Health & Happiness Clothing Market across from Sun Yatsen University
Between the two there has never been any ill will

You see fruit pits strewn over the sidewalks   gulp a new sweetheart and spit out love
The scenery of counter girls keeps changing
From dim sum brunches to midnight snacks   from arcade to outdoor food court
Streets are always being dug up and filled in   filled in and dug up
Bodies and tires are gradually wearing down
Staying alive   like a bowling ball rolling back and forth
The ground I've covered was only a short segment of road
Yet it passed through two eras   two overlapping worlds

1998
Translated by Denis Mair

A JOURNEY WITH NO DESTINATION

The airplane is the great bird of today, a shoe
a bridal palanquin flying through the air
there is no more distance between city N and city G
this so-called "long, drawn-out lifetime" will always be
as brief—*ah*—as a skirt slipping to the floor
when you leap from TV screens in the arrival lounge, caught by unseen cameras
I see your face like snow bared between far mountain peaks
just as I watched you vanish at the security gate not so long ago
it was as if you had turned around and come back
in the morning facing the mirror as you dress and do your makeup
and this action is regularly repeated thereafter
"It's as if I'd been here the whole time, leaving the ground only to come back down"
hermit crabs used to their new houses don't turn on any lights
the back of your tightly done-up dress is like the two halves of a Chinese door
gently opened, you're unpeeled
like a bamboo shoot
"Like an apple in autumn"
what links yesterday to today, memory with reality
is a narrow zipper
on the following day, a repeat performance
a modern reprint of an ancient parable: the hare and the tortoise
which of us will reach our destination first?
as the bus makes its way slowly and with difficulty
you drift above my head like a blank sheet of paper
the airplane flying over the low roof of the railway station once again

October 13, 1998
Translated by Simon Patton

THAT SLOWED-DOWN FEELING

cars swarm the streets like locusts
I hop to where I'm going like a huge flea on the city's skin
this mad dog "Busy" keeps snapping at my heels
these days
who doesn't go through life
like a wild rabbit?
in fact, I'd like to slow the pendulum of my mind   way down
slow . . . way . . . down . . .
I'd like to get a good grip on *something*
"I like that slowed-down feeling"
I hear your voice saying
at the Sunflower Bar, when things suddenly come to a halt
slow is a musical pause
the firm hold of reinforced steel on concrete
that beautiful unexpected stop when they shoot for goal
a book that takes three years to read
a two-minute nap in a meeting
hair in a mess—the second the breeze halts abruptly on the very tips of your hair
I'm only rushed off my feet because everyone else is
when things suddenly come to a halt
not excluding the sky-reddening sun, which drops with a *CRASH*
into nightlife overflowing with beer foam
"I like that slowed-down feeling"—completely relaxed
I hear your voice say that when you've just pulled back
and it makes me so glad
like a running shoe left by the side of the road

May 2, 1999
Translated by Simon Patton

WINDY BEIJING

Windy Beijing:
people on bikes
and startled sparrows everywhere
The thick air is filthy
The sun, trapped in haze,
is like a ruddy moon
Yesterday, only yesterday, we had clear autumn weather
Airborne paper   metaphysical, soaring
Plastic bags glide overhead   ballooned
so that I can see the form of the wind
Leaves rustle in trees
Covered from head to foot in dust, sparrows
fly twittering back to their nests
The ground is covered with Beijing accents
Thou, in whose unseen presence the buses and taxis are driven
Riding my bike, I
am like an arrow
taut against the bowstring
Fired into the Beijing wind
I shoot through the door of my rented house
Two policemen come knocking:
I remember as a boy,
reaching into a nest beneath a roof

November 24, 1999
Translated by Simon Patton

HUNAN GIRL, FLOWER GODDESS

bodies in tight clothes show voluptuous bumps
like frantic tiny animals no net can catch
in a scramble of crazy music
even God—head turned by lust—would rather live like a beast
but you hide away in a corner of passion
calm as a soundless red lotus flower
how tired your mind is
insouciantly removing long gloves thin as cicada wings from your naked arms
in your mind's eye, a pure lotus root pulled from slime
how gorgeous this endless wanton night is!
this city that knows no shame   pretty, coquettish flowers
In a fragmented age   who manages to keep body and soul intact?
who presumes to avoid the places where life happens
to avoid violence and injury?
black-smeared lips resembling a blood-red wound
pleasure is not reliable   it is nothing at all
the gyrating forms before me: so many blades of hollow-hearted grass
when you feel your body plummet in mid-glide
the hands of some hulking young man reach out spontaneously
this innocent maid—like a young swan dancing high above life—thinks with her body

December 31, 1999
Translated by Simon Patton

TAIYUAN CITY

In a haze of windblown dust I see the poet Lu Lu, alone
Passing Fourth Place near Nanhua Gate   a stroke of calligraphy ink
This is no illusion   at 3:15 in the afternoon
The weltering ground at his feet disperses like steam

A dust storm growls on the horizon, a pack of angry beasts
A pack deprived of a forest, scurrying about crazily
Like marauders entering a village
Lu Lu rounds a corner   a luminous streak through the pall

Keeps walking   a child accustomed to swallowing dirt
With inner grounds for sadness   hardly notices the murk around him
Even in fair weather   a kilo of leaden dust at the crown of his head
This final member of the gentry who bathes at dawn

"To hell with this weather!" he mutters
A sand dune obstructs his mellifluous throat
Right now he exudes a brand of liquor called "Fen"
Sunshine kindles in his belly   lines of poetry come on wings

I see him at 3:15, walking alone
With strong wingbeats like a wind-defying swallow
The world is being robbed of clarity by pelting grit
With imaginary scissors   tears snip out a patch of blue sky

April 19, 2000
Translated by Denis Mair

WHY DID THE CHICKEN CROSS THE ROAD?[*]

"A chicken . . . a road—I believe it was on this side to begin with."
Who ever thought we'd see a girl-chick so calm and composed?
(Why isn't it a rooster?)
Ignorant and fearless among the obnoxious cars
Going its way against the tide, at the bend
Of Zhongxiao East Road. The chicken's head
Bobs up and down, plotted to airy coordinates.
"That chicken is so joyful!"
"The chicken's intention is not a matter of the road,
          but of the landscape it passes through."
Sure enough, it has already passed through two gates
And the gentle grassy slope between.
The young chicken is carefree;
It saunters across the plush sod, aware that a landfill lies below.
A little earthworm (or a wad of stale gum)
Slips away several times.
"A chicken that doesn't want to cross roads is not a good chicken!"
When too many people travel it, no road is passable.
A thirty-meter crosswalk
Becomes a prolonged ordeal, like the Long March.
If the chick is not careful, it'll fall down a manhole with a missing cover.
(A little rooster is reflected in sewer water, making the girl-chick's blood flow faster.)
"Is that chicken throwing its life away?" No!
"That's clearly no chicken, it's a hero."
"To strive for the higher good . . ."
A line of footprints written like the word "no" [不]
Disappears in midair. It's like the Internet
At the moment when the connection is lost.
(Don't forget there is an egg, too
          if that chicken is a hen.)

Why did the chicken cross the road?
Why did the chicken cross the road?
(A chicken is too lowly to be crossing a highway, some would say
Said the chicken, "I insist on taking the high road, that's why.")

October 19, 2000
Translated by Denis Mair

---

* Quoted from "Why Did the Chicken Cross the Road," written collectively by web friends.

AT THE ZOO

No matter how large a cage is, it is still a cage
This   model prison
Wields the power to release its inmates   to an exercise yard
At that hour of the day
All the performers in the circus
Are put through their paces
An era of elephants and an era of ants
Are alike in paying honor to their God
An era of human beings
Installs a surveillance device
To monitor each tooth
All day a bare-assed monkey
Paces about with his genitals hanging
His only freedom is not wearing pants

The Manchurian tiger is a perfect beast
As it pounces on a trembling bantam rooster
Breakfast for a predator
Underneath that king-of-the-forest mask   is a slave being led about
Like wrestlers performing
Before a cheering audience
They summon up atavistic memories
Shot through with pangs of today's sorrow

The keeper extols the benefits to living things
Of eschewing money and hunts in the jungle
He gloatingly tells the citizens under him
This is the heavenly kingdom

A parrot that learned to speak complained
Said this human prison violates beastly principles
An eagle immediately drilled holes in its beak
And chained it shut that very day

A jaguar made a prison break
For a time snuck about in the city's private parts
But finding no cave to hole up in
It met a cruel fate again, this time under truck tires
In this overcrowded world
There is no safer refuge
Than within the walls of a prison

May 2001

Translated by Denis Mair

I CAME ACROSS A SMALL RICE FIELD IN DONGGUAN

Between the toes of factories
short-stemmed rice plants
clutch at the last bit of dirt
Their root-anchors
uncurl tiredly
Outraged hands   wanting to scratch
birdsong and cricket call from the mud
In a patch of gleaming sunlight
I saw rice-plant leaves
shrugging like shoulders
The spikes of rice grew quickly
The grains were in milk   They smiled faintly in the summer breeze
talking to me
All of a sudden, emerging from the impulsive oceanic din of notions
I wrung myself dry
like a white shirt
Yesterday, I would never have guessed
that in Dongguan
I could have come across a small field of rice
The yellow-green spikes
still swaying
through moments both happy and sad

May 2001
Translated by Simon Patton

THAT YEAR, WINTER

blade on blade, chill-chilling knives
in one night everything's cut clean away
city smothered in white cloth
bedroomless
stiffened trees, their branches ice-frigid limbs
those wending their way against the wind are
frail as blade on blade of grass
someone's single whispered cough
makes the roadside high-rise start

May 2001

Translated by Simon Patton

TURNING THAT SUNLIT SIDE OF HIS IN YOUR DIRECTION

he waits in brilliant sunlight
beside the crimson taxicab
for you
he resembles his country
dissembling
as if nothing has ever happened
it's now right at noon
even the architecture casts no shadows
all you see of him is his exterior
resembling the crab carried to your table
after approximately twenty minutes
in its hard outer casing
on the complimentary food platter
a solo persimmon sits
luscious   shiny
when you gently bite into it
it's then you find   that it's rotten inside
so great is your shock that you almost shout out loud
he doesn't bat an eyelid
and like the slice of apple beneath the knife
turns that sunlit side of his in your direction
the two of you part ways once more beneath bright sunshine
as if   nothing at all has changed
but you know   everything's utterly changed

August 20, 2001
Translated by Simon Patton

THE MISSING CAT

the cat's leaving was something predictable
nine-lived grimalkin
raised by fate in a prince's crumbling garden in Peking
in mud and snow, roaming alone

when it makes the train ride down south
it brings with it a rolling-rumbling great fog
just as that American poet I'm fond of, Carl Sandburg, once described it
(he and I share a love for fallen cities):
"The fog comes   on little cat feet"

from a fourth-floor balcony
the cat "sits looking
over harbor and city"
a door left open carelessly
and away it strays again:
"on silent haunches
and then moves on"

I have no worries for it
this grimalkin with its nine lives is indestructible
it's no doubt left for a brighter, more spacious place to be
gilt-silver cat-claws   shining, shining
ripping to shreds the entrails of some large bird

August 23, 2001
Translated by Simon Patton

A FEW MONKS STROLL DOWN LOVERS LANE

They are ambling along
Wind stirs ocean waves in their hundred-patch robes
Each is trying to get a word in edgewise
I can't catch the drift
As their mouths open to pronounce sounds
And the incoming tide banters with them
On Lovers Lane   no women walk at the monks' side
There is no sensual form
"Form is none other than emptiness"   sea and sky are a twin vastness
And the monks' mood is expansive
Their jug-eared heads are substantial in size
"Emptiness is none other than form"   a sculpted fishwife on yonder shoal
Wears a sheath dress with a pleat parted by waves
The scent of a woman's body pervades our lungs

Last night the woman I'm fond of walked here in front of me
By the sea, which is the opposite of a desert   *Ah*, Amitabha Buddha
In Iraq people are being killed
Tomahawks carry out "decapitation" strikes   Babylonian relics evaporate
Sakyamuni's disciples take their path outside of Christianity and Islam
How fortunate that the third road remains a road of peace
On this lazy afternoon
Monks stroll in springtime   while somewhere
The sardonic joke called SARS sneaks about like Saddam
Disease and war follow hard on mankind's heels
Like the shadows dogging those monks' footsteps
The recent respiratory illness is an "atypical syndrome"
Monks walking on Lovers Lane are an atypical sight
A few monks   a few gesticulating palm trees
Make a luminous partial view
In life's moody landscape painting

April 2003
Translated by Denis Mair

CHINESE PEOPLE

Those migrant workers who have to demand their wages.
148 pairs of battered hands
held out from Daqing's caved-in mine.
Li Aiye, who contracted AIDS after giving blood.
The shepherd bachelors of the loess slopes.
Gossipy women licking a finger to count money.
Hair salon girls: unlicensed sex workers.
Peddlers engaged in a running battle with city authorities.
Old bosses
in need of a sauna.
The nine-to-five tribe off to work on their bicycles.
Good-for-nothings with nowhere to go and nothing to do.
The barroom wasters. Old men
sipping tea as they pet songbirds.
Scholars who fill the heads of their listeners with fog.
Vagrants, punters, porters stinking to high heaven;
dandies, beggars, doctors, secretaries (and secret mistresses into the bargain);
workplace clowns
and other supporting actors.
From the Avenue of Heavenly Peace to the Guangzhou Road
I have yet to see "the Chinese people" this winter;
I've seen ordinary, speaking bodies
keeping each other warm
on buses day after day.
They're like grimy coins:
their users hand them over frowning
to society.

2004
Translated by Simon Patton

BOOKS OF SPRING ADRIFT

The beauty of knowledge lies in being transmitted.
                                        —theme of World Book Day

Each book is a precious bottle
Drifting on springtime's floodtide in brown eyes
Setting forth from spring   she runs, leaps
Up from the source of the heart's artesian well
Along the stream of fingers, the river of an arm
From you upstream   to him midstream   to me downstream
She can be slower than a spring breeze
Or faster than a spring rain
From a promenade, a bus stop, a construction site
To the door of a marital registry office
From the roar of a passenger jet at takeoff
To a subway that rolls through the seasons
Wherever this river passes, the faces are young

A book in its drifting course
Hauls up ancient Chinese characters on its way
Inscriptions on oracle bones and cauldrons   words on bamboo slips   in moveable clay type
Under different skies in different moods
On roads of different colors
Setting forth from the inner mind
Returning to the inner mind
Setting forth from springtime
Returning to springtime

Different motions and postures
Different ways of facing up to things
Each page of written words is a blade of grass, extending by degrees
Around it gorgeous pinks and purples of a meadow in flower

With a book in hand, face turned toward spring
Even the paralytic in his wheelchair
Stands upon the good earth
A deaf-mute hears and speaks with the heart's inner voice
Which disseminates more broadly than a river

A child born into ignorance goes journeying, lighter than a cloud
Cogitations of wise elders have the solidity of boulders
Wood begins to speak   stones bear flowers
The reckless lower their heads
The withered gain new life
The blind see reflections in a limpid river

Snow from a silent peak collapses and slides
Warmed by the ardor of life
The power of books
Is more powerful than any army

Go now, don't tell me you are just one drop
Don't tell me you are just a bottle
Afloat on a vast river
Wherever water's purling fingers are at work
The red cord of life is crafted
Into scarlet creations of macramé

Into the distance   into the river of knowledge
Drifting ever onward in the freshets of our brown eyes[*]

April 21, 2005
Translated by Denis Mair

---

* This poem was commissioned for the tenth World Book Day. As part of the "Books Adrift in Spring"
  celebration on April 23, performers led more than a thousand people in reading it aloud on the grass
  slope in front of Guangzhou National Library.

IN A POMEGRANATE, I SEE THE MOTHERLAND

In a pomegranate, I see the motherland
Plump colossal fruit of heaven and earth
Within itself holding progeny that stick together
Naked skin protecting its crystal-clear heart
Children joining hands in multitudes
At a branch's end its smile is sweet and tart
In the season of fruitfulness   *Ah*, a birthing couch for a mother-to-be
I wish to remember each window of October

To stroke the pomegranate's yellow membrane
Is to stroke the motherland's fresh new growth
I see the provinces neighboring each other
The sunrise-facing east side of one   is next to another's sunset-facing side
I see highland daughters, wearing garlands in their hair
Each oval face is ruddy, and young women standing tall
Are wearing skirts of pomegranate hue
Their pomegranate lips are juicy red

I also see that the pomegranate has split open
Some brothers are dining on wind, sleeping in the dew
Ah, my dearly beloved brothers
Their indomitable backs, knobby and earth-colored
Bearing the hardships of crevice-riddled soil
Each vein standing out is a mark of hard toil
I find that their cracked hands repay careful scrutiny
I find that their creases are silent cries
Across the land, painful shouts stimulate leaves
To grow madly in the spring wind
Trunks and branches rise to the occasion
To put forth interlocking limbs and twigs
And proffer flower clusters with vaulting élan
Made up of florets that are light and yet seem heavy
Like flames that aren't snuffed out by pouring rain
Floral wind chimes to shake the dawn awake

Before the lion-maned sun grew old
This fruit commenced its branch-tip dance
Within a dream's splendor I stand and gaze
At each sky-aiming pomegranate tree
Each tree like a citizen with bowed waist
Holding forth a red heart, wrested from within itself
On its well-proportioned frame hang a treeful of citizens

2006

Translated by Denis Mair

RELATED AND UNRELATED

Avian flu is related to chickens and ducks
Type A influenza is unrelated to pigs [so don't call it swine flu]
The relation of SARS to civet cats remains ambiguous
This is not a medical question, it is a sin foisted on animals by articulate humans
Swiping a book is not stealing   potatoes are not the same as French fries
A downturn can be dignified with the name of negative growth
Inarticulate animals can't find a lawyer to defend their innocence

9/11 is not related to Al-Qaeda   Hezbollah may or may not be related to *inshallah*
We're not sure if recent bomb blasts in Afghanistan are related to Bin Laden
Bin Laden must be a civet cat, the way he holes up in caves and hollow trees
Keeping company with armadillos and moles   lying low by day and coming out at night
To deal with him, Americans have to change into beasts themselves   What do you make of that!
Out on the street, an American spy satellite can spot the second hand on a girl's "Swatch"
But for some reason Bin Laden's wristwatch still eludes their cameras

Iraq is related to major oil fields   Saddam has nothing to do with weapons of mass destruction
Between Obama's peace prize and George Dubya, there must be a distant blood tie
If Little Bush hadn't been so gung ho for war, Obama could not have been a peacemaker
Europeans were sitting on this bundle of old money from dynamite
Then they awarded it to the nation that intervenes all over the world
What a knee-slapper!
Expanding armaments is for peace   anti-terror is to end war
A few days ago, two migrant workers were coughing on a bus
I'm talking about the "Chinese worker"—who almost got picked as *Time*'s "Man of the Year"
They were given a unanimous cold shoulder by the other passengers
In this country, lots of people pretend they want nothing to do with democracy
Yet sometimes they have to invoke this magnificent-sounding name
While dealing with people more disadvantaged than themselves

December 24, 2009
Translated by Denis Mair

FRIEND IN THE BLOGOSPHERE

Concealed on the far side of the screen
Fishlike submersion

You
Are unreachable   farther than far

I cannot see your face
Your pupils   your bones   your gleaming scales

It's like plunging into a mile-high fogbank
Virtual sounds   whispers are whisked away by wind

Message window   comments   notes in box
At any time your words may leap into view
Specks that resolve through wreathing mist
Drips and drops convey a heartbeat's strength   build to a downpour

My interpretations   like the lake's surface where raindrops drum
Making dimples of *déjà vu*

Seen on the surface, these blade-like fins have a familiar look
Still unmet but feeling connected

Being sized up this way   makes me fear I'll prove unworthy
An encounter in the virtual world
Flames burning underwater

March 26, 2010
Translated by Denis Mair

BIG

Utah, here I am!   Salt Lake Desert, here I am!

I am cleansed by your expanse of white blankness

I've accrued a debt of exactly one drop

    because the Chinese word "lake" [湖] is written with water [氵]

And around it should grow a mustache [胡] of watercress

    with flecks of light dancing on waves [波]

In one eon you accomplished the conversion from liquid to solid

Now in granular form stretching out of sight

       much nicer than Death Valley's brackish puddles

Can this debt ever be cleared up by Farnsworth Peak and the Wasatch Mountains?

Wouldn't you say Salt Lake Valley is a limnological luminary   a lake among lakes?

English speakers would say it's the "salt of the earth"

When it all seems too much for words   time to get behind the wheel

Spend a day driving huge circles on the flats

"It's time you went home"—Even Niagara Falls starts to urge me

"You are not Emily Dickinson   you are not José Heredia

Only their waterfall poems could avail themselves of such fateful vertical drops"

Here I am   for those who missed out on the Chinese language since the nineteenth century!

Auden is very much with me in 2012   so tell me   why would I want to be naturalized?

Before the American egg was fertilized   Li Bai rode rapids dropping ten thousand feet in one day

Not quite a year ago I was trekking   to where the Yellow River descends from the sky

Like in a Hollywood blockbuster   I was a leading man who still lacked an adversary

Rising in a gyre over my country's brave new era   the Empire State Building is not so dizzying

I assume my own stance   just as Guangzhou Tower did

Under a vast, profound sky   the tower sprang upright, as if in a fever

Yet it lacks the history and height I am looking for

Colorado, here I am!   Rocky Mountains, here I am!

From deep in a chasm   I leap to the platform of a peak

Viewing 300 million square kilometers of the Great Plains

The word "big" cannot do it justice

You're a superpower!   Your GNP exceeds twenty percent of the world's total!

Leave me some grounds for MY big ego   it doesn't have to be politics or the economy

I'm here   at the intersection of Fifth Avenue and Broadway

In front of a Latino lady with curves in all the right places, like a yeasty bun

At the foot of a skyscraper, let me add Americans to my series "The People"

In San Francisco's Chinatown, there are door plaques in block characters

Along a whole street, the motherland appears as my mother tongue

One big-bruiser truck after another zooms by at life-or-death speeds

Bulked-up Ford sedans muscle their way into the traffic stream

Ezra Pound, I'm here to shout it   our kind did not just crawl out of huts
It's time for a new chapter in the East-West clash of wits
In our errant course you and I have met at a defile
      now I'm of an age for a grudge match

John Ashbery, I'm here   New York, I'm here
Evoke the biggest prairie you can, Dickinson   I'm here
Langston Hughes, I'm here   state of Mississippi, I'm here
William Carlos Williams   I'm here, pushing a red wheelbarrow
Carl Sandburg, I'm here   Chicago of the broad shoulders, I'm here
Occident, Orient, tell me   who owes a debt to whom?
For 172 years I've hated you   now I break the mold and approach you as a friend
In Walt Whitman's lines, I learned about romantic Long Island
In Ginsberg's howl, I met a hipster generation that doesn't give a damn
In Chinese, *Dada* sounds like "big, big"   I'm here on the big, big American road
What other milestones of alternate space-time can you show?
Fleeting lives pave a roadway for epics   this year I'm in my prime
Brooklyn Bridge   Mississippi   Yellowstone   they all pay their respects along my way
Ahoy to the Pacific on my left, to Arizona, Rhode Island, and New Hampshire
They step forward by turns to greet me   Ahoy to the Atlantic on my right
It's a tilt-a-whirl world   *New Yorker, Time,* the *Wall Street Journal* have no time to report on me
History is written by rubber tires   Uncle Sam has been retreating ahead of me

The ancients built Bronze Mynah Tower in Ye City [where Li Bai backed the wrong prince]
      towers were places to sound the heavens
      and today I'm leaving my answer in Phoenix
Hail the bigness of the sun!   I sing of the Great Yangtze bearing all eastward
      to measures of Su Dongpo's prosody
Hail the Western phoenix!   *Ah,* banished immortal   I commandeer the Garuda of his rhapsody
      to lyricize Times Square anew
My squandered intervals come back in daylight savings of five time zones
From my dynasties before the Common Era   my Han and Tang   my Song, Yuan, Ming, Qing
From my 1966   and my 1978   and now here in 2012
Big canyon   big waterfall   big prairie   big salt flat   big hit films
Along with your American driver driving a big "Transformer"™ truck
It's all so super big   freedom, democracy, the Constitution   yes—big, big, big
But your bigs are receding   I'm revved up to cover serious distance   history slopes upward
The sky soon opens to my peak-mounting expectations   time is being dwarfed
In my excitement I discover   the government is too small
A big hornet has stung me awake with a screaming steel needle!

2012

Translated by Denis Mair

LET THAT FOOTBALLER BE PRIME MINISTER

Men running across the playing field
Create a new Greek legend
Roaring Karagounis is the passionate Homer for today
He is the soul of the people
Having represented the national team a record 120 times
He has no fear of going out yet again
Amid the shouts and cheering of his fans, he seems to be prime minister
The earth is round, and he circles it to fulfill his dream
And perhaps roll over the depressed economy
All this for Aphrodite
The beauty in the stands who paints her face blue
He will fight to the last breath

His head coach, Bosque, could be the finance minister of Spain
The essence of his no-forward strategy is to maintain control
As gears mesh smoothly in a well-oiled engine
His players do their work in perfect order
But the gorgeous footwork, powerful passing
Intense attacks won't be enough; winning is what matters
He has what it takes to lead his men
Quick cut-in passes show the acumen of a top investor
Fans do the wave through the stands, up and down
Without a thought for the rise and fall of the euro
National boundaries give way to a green playing field
Europe comes charging with the ball
Goal!
Those staring at the TV screen jump for joy
Their passion brings the wrangling of state leaders to a standstill.

2012
Translated by Ning Yang

NOWADAYS HIGH-RISES ARE THE CROPS OF THE CITY

Vying for land with rice   vying for land with corn
Vying for land with soybeans and sorghum
Vying for land with folks who dwell in old buildings
Nowadays high-rises are the crops of the city

Rice plants in rural villages get shorter all the time
Two kinds of crops are being painfully left behind
Grandparents, straggly and lurching   kids weathering a dry season
The city cuts deep furrows   strews seeds across them
Buildings spring up like stalks, adding height each day
Porches, penthouses, landscaped estates at your window
Greenery ready to flower, brought in half-grown from nurseries

The soil belongs to the state   the state belongs to the people
But the high-and-mighty state seems to have no handle on the soil
It seems unrelated to those myrmidons who are busy filling their bellies
Thunk! A big seal stamped on a document who-knows-where
Sets the snowball of wealth rolling for certain people
The developer signs for rights to a really big plot
        with borrowed funds he can hire workers to till it
Skillful planting is still done by farmers   as day labor or on contract
Now they have donned hard hats
Grain prices keep climbing   agencies and brokers rake in cash
On the escalator of merit   big money always wins promotions
The city's crops block out the sun and sky
Swarms of people dart among the roots, on foot and wheels
Like leeches, earthworms, and tadpoles
We like to say the land's worth is measured in gold
How grand these gold-plated houses as thick as a comb's teeth
Where common people can't even afford a snail-shell home!

Those who face gentrification watch over ancestral paddies
A high wind is blowing in the sky as the economy slumps
Large-scale developers shout their misery to the heavens
All day with tireless zeal they keep tilling this field of new hope

2012
Translated by Denis Mair

SLINKY WAIST[*]

How could Bai Juyi's beloved "Slinky Waist"
Ever compare with our lithe, slender southern beauty?
A streak of effulgence   like a fairy maiden coaxed to earth
The Pearl River prostrates itself before her feet
Ready to be gathered into her arms

In an era that values the statuesque in women
Even the sveltest of ladies may go on a diet
A rosebud mouth is more striking than Juliet's painted lips
It would require quite a giant
To hold Slinky Waist in his arms
Or a distant cloud would have to descend

A sprinkling of stars in the fall sky
Sets off her lovely brow
From where can you see her lissome figure?
Hah! Along the panorama of Pearl River
The whole city of Guangzhou
Is the dimple of her smile

2012
Translated by Denis Mair

---

[*] Citizens of Guangzhou have nicknamed the Guangzhou Tower "Slinky Waist," which was the name the
Tang poet Bai Juyi gave to his favorite courtesan.

STONE

1.

Sole original presence   molten fluid from a huge fire
Within the body of the world   swirling in currents of lava
Stone is the totality of mineral matter
The awkward skeleton of Planet Earth
Omnipresent
Devastation forced stone to give birth to stone
Heaping millions of huge stones into towering ranges
Fragmenting big stones into countless pebbles
In loose dirt it takes another form
Dao gives birth to One   One gives birth to two   two gives birth to three
        three to myriads of things
Cobblestones and cicadas and toadstools

2.

Poems are nothing but sentences constructed of stone
A struck flint shoots a star-like spark
Civilization spreads like a grassfire   once started, it won't stop
An infant goes down a road paved with stones   heading toward a grave
Megaliths watch over the land's hard-bitten silence
Time is surrounded on all sides
Stone foundation, stone wall, stone pillar
People are poetically dwelling   stones feel nothing within
Conspiring with the remote past, cement is a modern mutation of stone
And cremated remains of stone are used to whitewash walls
Wavering at the edge of birth and death   existing for the sake of existence

3.

The greatest adventure is to go inside a stone
Like dinosaurs of the Cretaceous period
Handing themselves over to custodians of eternity
Once it has swum into a solidified sea, a fish's swishing tail
Is the most deceptive treatment of life

Stone possessing beauty is jade   in the Orient rivaling the superior man's dignity
Collect a stone only when struck by its presence   be a connoisseur of stones   to nurture your spirit
Relish the feel of mountains and valleys in the palm of your hand
Soil of the native land
Depends upon the heart's Gibraltar

Gem-like words   emerge from a swarthy inkstone   carved in grotesque designs
With apparent murkiness it gives utterance
To the cleansing of a soul

4.

A basalt cave is the uterus of creation
Scenery is born from stone   craggy terrain is the manifestation of stone
The appeal of a landscape lies in the ugliness of stone   great obduracy is wisdom
On the blackest crags   bleakness lifts its bracingly bleak face

Off to the side of time   shoals seem to gaze out to sea
Insinuating teeth of wind   undistracted tongue of waves
By long attrition   gnaw a pitted beauty into shape
There is bewitchment in being utterly shattered
What they call "Ocean Corner, Edge of Sky"   is nothing but a pile of stones*

2012

Translated by Denis Mair

---

* "Ocean Corner, Edge of Sky" (Tianya-haijiao) is the name of a rock formation in Sanya City, Hainan
 Province. Numerous boulders are strewn along the beach, all of them dramatically contorted in shape.

FATEFUL AS EVER, OUR MEETING IN CHINA

The sky dispatches a cloudburst to add excitement
At the podium I recite Zagajewski's "Chinese Poem"
In tribute to a poet who sits among us tonight
Fleeting as always is our time in China   bright as ever is lightning from abroad

A strong flash from overhead collides with light from my own eyes
A momentary blink shows objects acid-etched
Lit from behind by life's ruddy glare of history
Is it by coincidence?
I just imagined raindrops splashing on Song roof tiles
Plinking on rims of blue-flower porcelain from the Ming
And just now through the blue eyes of a Polish poet
A poet from my country's past was seen boating on a southern river
Nightlong rain danced on transparent tiptoes atop the boat's awning
His murmured words slipped into the river's current
Trackless like a white bird skimming over the waves
The empire was strife-torn   only the poet's heart was at peace
Face illumined by a white porcelain lamp
Through the haze I cannot tell   is that Xin Qiji or Su Shi
Or some other well-known lyricist of the Song?
With freshets of rain pouring down along my way
I am swept into an onrushing confluence
As if in a submarine   in a locomotive with a cowcatcher
Parting the current, taking a watery road
I am like a fish swimming into recesses of time
As I learn what our expansive era makes possible
From Krakow all the way to Guangzhou City
Poets from disparate lands meet in one "field"
On a light-flooded stage   so many years fall away
The rain's thousand-year patter has not weakened
Storm clouds roll in, as always, from abroad   fateful as ever is our meeting in China
In this moment of pealing thunder   let the trance not be broken
Is that chanting we hear from the sky's edge   a sound like pouring rain?

April 3, 2014
Translated by Denis Mair

TWO HALVES OF THE WORLD APPLE

1.

I awake at dawn on the West Coast
As you enter dark night in the Orient
Planet Earth is the letter "O"
It resembles an apple   a ball struck by God's bat
Sent on a spinning course through the cosmos
I toy with this metaphor so suited to Amerika
Yet I embrace my country's way of Taiji
in which the contrary poles of something
Are yin and yang fish chasing each other's tails
When I keep you in mind, I see this more clearly

What looms before my eyes are two pine trees
Trunks coiled with tensile strength   solidified shapes of storm
Ten thousand golden threads come through a sieve of needles
Casting gleams on water in a shallow pond
The green feathers of two wild ducks catch the morning light

2.

I stroll on a puncheon trail down by the shore
Waves make the sea's skin white   the world slowly opens
The sky melts in pellucid depth   milky clouds spill across it
Past the sun's suspended medallion
As I reach the turn-in to Estate No. Eight
Again it comes back to me—the friendly *Hi, hi*
Of two buxom black girls, blended with seagull cries
Ringing out over the blue expanse of seawater
Reaching the globe's other half in an instant
The distance from sunrise to sunset
Has to pass through a gauntlet of barriers
Right now the next block's streetlight is getting closer
Amid the hubbub of a meat and produce market
We walk by leaning together like two verdant leeks

A raised walkway yellows like paper in somnolent heat
Until the velvety skin of night is cooled by a footloose wind
Pale brow of moon and eyes of stars
Light filters into every corner
A grouse somewhere clucks twice
A text message from you
Swims the Pacific like a whale
In the palm of my hand   the Eastern and Western Hemispheres
Are so near   like the girl next door

May 2014
Translated by Denis Mair